How Can I Help?
Friends Helping Friends™

HELPING A FRIEND WITH AN
ALCOHOL PROBLEM

Jennifer Landau

ROSEN
PUBLISHING

New York

Published in 2017 by The Rosen Publishing Group, Inc.
29 East 21st Street, New York, NY 10010

First Edition

Library of Congress Cataloging-in-Publication Data

Names: Landau, Jennifer, 1961– author.
Title: Helping a friend with an alcohol problem / Jennifer Landau.
Description: First edition. | New York : Rosen Publishing, 2017. | Series: How can I help? Friends helping friends | Includes bibliographical references and index.
Identifiers: LCCN 2016017405| ISBN 9781499464504 (library bound) | ISBN 9781499464481 (pbk.) | ISBN 9781499464498 (6-pack)
Subjects: LCSH: Teenagers—Alcohol use—Juvenile literature. | Alcoholism—Juvenile literature. | Alcoholism—Treatment—Juvenile literature.
Classification: LCC HV5135 .L356 2017 | DDC 362.2920835—dc23
LC record available at https://lccn.loc.gov/2016017405

Manufactured in China

CONTENTS

INTRODUCTION

By your teenage years, you've likely been exposed to alcohol through family or friends, at home or at house parties. According to a 2014 survey by the Substance Abuse and Mental Health Services Administration (SAMHSA), by age fifteen 35 percent of teens have had at least one drink and by age eighteen that number jumps to 65 percent.

In 2014, 8.7 million young people ages twelve to twenty reported they drank alcohol beyond "just a few sips" in the previous month. In addition, according to the SAMHSA survey young people who start drinking before age fifteen are five times more likely to become dependent on alcohol than those who start drinking at twenty-one. What's even scarier is that many of those young people are binge drinkers, which is defined as drinking four or more drinks within two hours if you're a woman and five or more drinks in the same amount of time if you're a man.

When you drink to excess, your motor skills, muscle control, depth perception, and vision are impaired. You make poor decisions, too, like taking part in risky sexual behavior and driving drunk or being a passenger in the car of someone who's been drinking. You might even be risking your life. According to the Centers for Disease Control and Prevention (CDC) more than 4,300 young people die every year as a result of underage drinking. This figure includes car crashes, homicides, drowning deaths, and suicides. In

If you have a friend who drinks to excess, you might feel conflicted about the best way to help her deal with her drinking problem.

addition, a report from SAMHSA stated that in 2010 there were about 189,000 alcohol-related emergency room visits by young people under the age of twenty-one.

Over time, heavy drinking can result in damage to your brain and body, making you more vulnerable to cancer, liver disease, and other conditions. You can also become physically dependent on alcohol, which requires intensive medical and psychological treatment. Drinking under the age of twenty-one is also illegal in all fifty U.S. states, so those who drink could find themselves in trouble with the law. Of course, the only way to avoid all these problems is not to drink.

Maybe you don't drink yourself, but are worried about a friend who drinks too much. If you think a friend is abusing alcohol, it's easy to feel conflicted. You want to help, but don't know where to turn. A great place to start is to arm yourself with knowledge about alcohol and how it affects the mind and body. As you read on, you'll learn about the reasons your friend might drink and the signs that your friend has an alcohol problem. You'll learn how to best approach her and how to take care of yourself in the process, including bringing others on board to help as you go through this difficult situation. Treatment options are discussed, as are ways for you to get involved in the fight against alcohol and drug abuse by joining groups such as Students Against Destructive Decisions (SADD). Most important, you'll see that there is hope for your friend and for those who love her.

CHAPTER ONE

DRINKING DAMAGE

I f someone drinks too much alcohol, you may say that he is drunk or wasted or lit. "Intoxicated" or "inebriated" are more formal terms used to describe being influenced by alcohol to the extent that it's hard to control your mind or your body. No matter what words you use, when you drink alcohol to excess you put yourself—and others—in danger.

So what is alcohol, anyway? The alcohol people drink is a drug called ethyl alcohol, which is made by a process known as fermentation. Fermentation is a chemical change whereby microorganisms act on the sugar and starch in products such as fruit, grains, and potatoes. During fermentation, these products mix with yeast, which breaks down the sugar and releases carbon dioxide and ethyl alcohol. There are other types of alcohol, such as those found in nail polish and paint thinners, but they are toxic in even small amounts and should never be ingested.

SETTING THE STANDARD

In the United States, a standard-size drink contains 0.6 fluid ounces (18 milliliters) of pure alcohol. Examples of standard-size drinks include one 12-ounce (355-ml) beer, 8 to 9 ounces (237-266 ml) of malt liquor, 5 ounces (148 ml) of table wine, and 1.5 fluid ounces (44 ml) of drinks such as gin, rum, vodka, and the like. By point of comparison, a 16-ounce (473 ml) can of malt liquor contains two drinks and a bottle of wine contains five drinks.

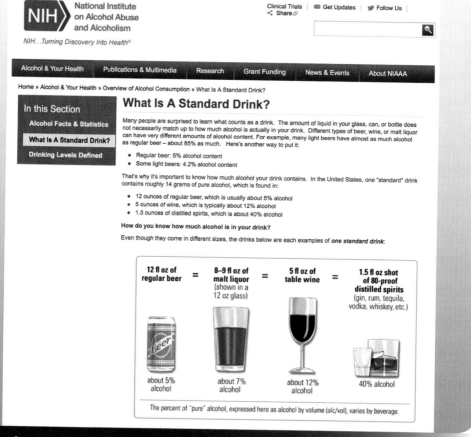

According to the National Institute on Alcohol Abuse and Alcoholism (https://www.niaa.nih.gov), in the United States there are about 14 grams (0.50 ounce) of pure alcohol in a standard-size drink.

Among teens who drink, binge drinking is the norm, which means they are having many standard-size drinks in a short amount of time. There are even those who practice extreme binge drinking by having ten or more drinks on one occasion. Another dangerous activity is mixing alcohol and energy drinks, which contain a lot of caffeine. This caffeine boost prevents someone from feeling as drunk as he really is and can lead to even heavier drinking.

EASILY ADDICTED

According to the CDC, young people use and abuse alcohol more than any other drug. Alcohol is a highly addictive drug, which means it is easy to become psychologically and physically dependent on it. When you drink, your brain releases dopamine and endorphins, chemicals that bring pleasure and reduce pain. These good feelings make you want to drink more and more to keep your brain satisfied. For people over age twenty-one who drink a moderate amount, alcohol can help them feel relaxed or at ease in social situations. It's an easy drug to abuse, however, which can lead someone into the danger zone.

Alcohol is a psychoactive drug, which means it brings about changes in mood, behavior, and consciousness. It is classified as a depressant, a type of psychoactive drug that interferes with the functioning of the central nervous system. Messages from nerve receptors to the brain get blocked, resulting in reduced brain activity. When the brain activity is reduced, it affects everything from the person's perceptions to his moods to his physical

When an individual drinks, the brain releases chemicals that can make that person feel good at first, but over time it will take more and more alcohol to keep the brain satisfied.

movements. Despite the name, depressants do not make someone feel depressed, at least not at first. If someone drinks heavily, in time this behavior can lead to symptoms of depression, with or without an underlying mental illness.

FEELING THE EFFECTS

As soon as you start drinking, your body begins to absorb alcohol into your bloodstream. The alcohol is then carried through the bloodstream to your brain, liver, kidney, and other internal organs. How intoxicated you become depends on the amount of alcohol in your bloodstream.

A way to measure the level of drunkenness is by means of the blood alcohol concentration (BAC). If someone has a BAC of 0.08, for example, he or she has eight parts of alcohol for every thousand parts of blood. In the United States, a BAC of 0.08 is the legal definition of intoxicated. A person's BAC is determined by means of a blood or urine test or by using a device called a breathalyzer that measures the amount of alcohol in someone's breath.

Alcohol is metabolized in the liver, but the liver can break down only a small amount of alcohol at a time, leaving the rest to move throughout the body. If you are binge drinking there is no way your body can break down the alcohol as fast as you are consuming it.

A breathalyzer measures a person's blood alcohol concentration (BAC) by means of a breath test. In the United States, a person is legally intoxicated if he has a BAC of 0.08.

There are several factors that influence how quickly alcohol affects a particular person. These factors include the person's weight, how much she has eaten, and just how fast those drinks are being consumed. Female bodies process alcohol differently from male bodies (and females tend to weigh less) so it is likely they will become inebriated at a faster rate.

SERIOUS CONSEQUENCES

If your friend is drunk, he may slur his words or stumble around or say things that are offensive, often in a loud voice. People who drink also make some very poor decisions. Drinking lowers your inhibitions, so your friend is more likely to take offense over some comment and pick a fight. The fight might start out with hurt feelings and harsh words, but it could lead to physical violence. Teens who drink are more likely to engage in risky sexual behavior such as having unprotected sex or sex with multiple partners. There is also the increased likelihood that a teen will drink and drive or get a ride with someone who is also intoxicated.

Teen girls might be at a particular risk. Not only can unprotected sex lead to an unwanted pregnancy, but according to the National Institute on Alcohol Abuse and Alcoholism (NIAAA), ninety-seven thousand students between the ages of eighteen and twenty-four are victims of alcohol-related sexual assault. Although the majority of those cases are young women, it is not unheard of for a young man to be the victim of sexual assault. There is an increased risk for assault when both the victim and the abuser used alcohol before the attack.

Underage drinking could also lead to legal trouble. Each state has its own laws, but if someone under the age of twenty-one gets caught drinking she could be taken into custody and forced to enter an alcohol treatment program.

Get caught with a fake ID to buy alcohol and you could be hit with jail time or a hefty fine. There might even be a conviction on your permanent record, which could lead to trouble getting a job or gaining admission into college. Drinking and driving also leaves a black mark on your record and could lead to suspension of your license, fines, and mandatory attendance in drug and alcohol and driver's education classes, as well as community service.

If parents or guardians get caught allowing those who are underage to drink on their property they could face legal action, too. In addition, buying alcohol for someone under the age of twenty-one is illegal in all fifty states.

YOUR BRAIN ON ALCOHOL

A teenager's brain is not yet fully formed. Scientists now believe that the brain doesn't stop developing until a person is in his mid-twenties or early thirties. The fact that a teen's brain is still maturing means he can have difficulty with certain neurological functions. It may be hard for him to make informed decisions, for example, or to see what problems might arise in the future. These issues with neurological functioning can lead to poor choices when it comes to alcohol use.

Binge drinking or chronic alcohol use is dangerous because these actions keep areas of the brain from developing properly. The hippocampus, which is the part of the

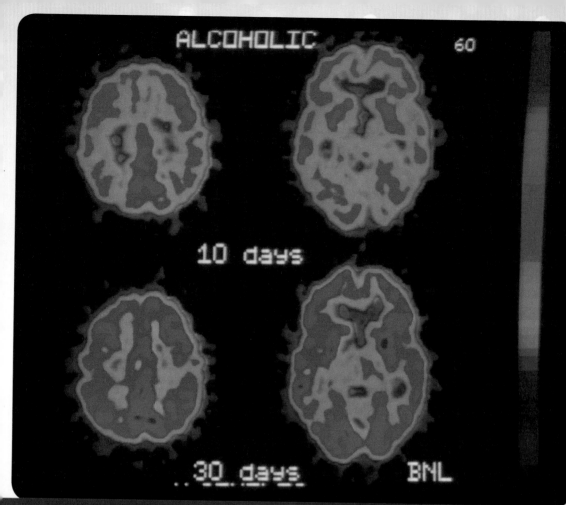

ALCOHOLIC   60

10 days

30 days   BNL

This brain scan shows the increase in brain activity (highlighted in yellow) as someone goes from ten days without alcohol (*top row*) to thirty days without alcohol (*bottom row*).

brain that regulates working memory and learning, is negatively affected by alcohol. When alcohol reaches your hippocampus you can have trouble remembering something you just learned like an address or phone number. Excessive alcohol use can lead to a blackout, which is not being able to remember large chunks of time, including what you did the previous night. The prefrontal cortex, which is responsible for planning ahead and using good judgment, can also be

14

damaged by alcohol use, as can the cerebellum, which controls motor coordination, among other things.

In 2010, neuroscientist Susan Tapert ran a study comparing the brain scans of teens who drank to excess with those who didn't drink. Tapert discovered that those who drank heavily had damaged nerve tissue, or white matter, in their brain. "They appeared to have a number of little dings throughout their brains' white matter, indicating poor quality," Tapert told National Public Radio. The binge drinkers also performed worse on tests of memory and thinking.

ALCOHOL POISONING

Drinking a lot of alcohol in a short amount of time can lead to alcohol poisoning, which is an emergency situation. Excessive alcohol use can affect a person's breathing, body temperature, heart rate, and blood sugar level. Alcohol irritates the stomach so severe vomiting can occur. This effect is particularly dangerous because alcohol abuse suppresses the gag reflex, which is what prevents someone from choking on his own vomit. It's not easy to think of your friend in such an extreme circumstance, but you should know the signs of alcohol poisoning. These include mental confusion, vomiting, seizures, low body temperature, pale or bluish skin color, and passing out.

Don't think that your friend can just "sleep it off." The only thing that works to lessen the effects of alcohol is time, but if someone is suffering from alcohol poisoning you don't have time to wait. Without treatment, alcohol poisoning can lead to coma and even death. It's always better to be overly

HANGOVERS

Hangovers hurt. When you have a hangover, you usually have a splitting headache and are nauseous and weak and dizzy. You might sweat a lot and feel thirsty. Hangovers happen after you drink too much alcohol. As a rule, the more alcohol you use, the worse your symptoms will be, although there's no way to know how much you can drink and still avoid a hangover. There are some things that make it more likely that you'll have a hangover or that it will be more severe. These factors include:

- Using other drugs along with alcohol

- Drinking on an empty stomach

- Getting a bad night's sleep after drinking

- Drinking darker colored alcohol, which contains a chemical more likely to produce hangovers

Hangovers are typically at their worst when your blood alcohol concentration returns back down to zero. Once they start they can last for up to twenty-four hours. There are no cures for a hangover other than time, but drinking plenty of water to avoid dehydration and taking an over-the-counter pain reliever to ease the headache might help. Of course, the best way to avoid the pain of a hangover is not to drink at all.

cautious, so if you think your friend is in immediate danger, call 911. Stay with your friend and if he is awake, try to keep him up. If your friend needs to lie down, make sure he is on his side to avoid choking on his vomit.

BODILY HARM

Long-term heavy drinking can cause a whole host of health problems. Someone who abuses alcohol is at risk for heart disease, pancreatitis, which is inflammation of the pancreas, and a range of cancers, including those that affect the mouth, throat, larynx, esophagus, and liver. The liver is particularly vulnerable because it is the organ that breaks down alcohol. When alcohol is broken down it releases toxins that can damage liver cells. Over time, scar tissue

This photo shows, from left to right, the stages of liver disease. When you drink to excess, your liver cells are damaged, and over time scar tissue builds up.

builds up and when that tissue begins to take over most of the liver the result is a condition called cirrhosis. Symptoms of cirrhosis include fatigue, confusion, nausea, loss of appetite, and bruising or bleeding easily. There is no cure for cirrhosis, but you can prevent it from getting worse by giving up drinking. If too much scar tissue builds up, your liver could fail and you would need a transplant.

Alcohol is also harmful for a developing fetus. There is no completely safe level of alcohol use for a pregnant woman, and drinking heavily during pregnancy can result in a baby developing fetal alcohol syndrome (FAS). Babies born with FAS often have abnormal facial features and small heads, as well as heart defects and central nervous system problems, including cognitive deficits and attention issues. Because heavy drinking makes it more likely that someone will have unprotected sex, an unplanned pregnancy—and one that puts the baby in peril because of alcohol use—is a real cause for concern.

CHAPTER TWO

STRONG INFLUENCES

The teenage years are a time of great change. Teenage bodies are growing and developing. Teens have more schoolwork and other responsibilities, such as driving or holding down an afterschool job. They are striving for independence, too, and spending less time with parents and more time alone or with friends. The need for excitement and adventure is at a high level and emotions are intense. Teens are also searching for their own identity separate from their family and dealing with growing romantic and sexual interests. This transition to adulthood is part of life, but the stress of all these changes can make someone more likely to turn to alcohol.

MANY REASONS WHY

There are many reasons why a teenager may drink. At first, drinking might seem like a way to have fun, to party with friends or just escape the everyday. A teen may turn to alcohol to deal with a difficult circumstance, such as her parents' divorce or a painful breakup.

Some teens drink to deal with difficult emotions such as depression or anxiety. Drinking alcohol might offer relief for a short time, but can lead to alcohol abuse.

For some, boredom could be a factor. Teens who have a hard time being alone and a strong need for excitement are prime candidates for substance abuse. A 2013 study by researchers at Carnegie Mellon University and the University of Pittsburgh found that teenagers who drink alone are more likely to drink as a way to deal with negative emotions.

A desire to rebel against what your parents expect of you and to act more like an adult—and like your peers—can also make you more likely to drink. There might be an underlying mental illness such as depression or anxiety, and self-medicating with alcohol may make those uncomfortable feelings go away for a short time. According to the National Alliance on Mental Illness (NAMI) about a third of all people with mental illness—and half with more severe mental illness—also abuse alcohol, so there is a need for caution among this population.

THE POWER OF PEERS

Maybe you've been in a situation where a group of your peers is pushing you to do something you know is wrong, like skip class or cheat on a test. When a peer is pushing you to act a certain way that is known as peer pressure. Peer pressure can be positive (for example, encouraging someone to try out for a sport), or negative. When it comes to drinking, one person can try to persuade another by saying things such as "It's no big deal" or "Don't ruin the party." It can be hard to resist this type of pressure. You might worry about being rejected or teased. You don't want to hurt someone's feelings. You might not know how to get yourself or your friend out of a tough spot.

It can be awkward to go against peer pressure, but there are things you can say to avoid drinking. Remind your friends that you're driving and don't want to wreck your car. Say that your parents would go ballistic if they knew you were drinking. Tell them your coach would kick you off the team if he found out. Another option is to tell them that you've decided not to drink and you'd like their support. If they are true friends, they'll stand behind your decision.

PARENTAL GUIDANCE

Although it sometimes might seem as if teens and their parents have little common ground, parents have a big impact on their children's alcohol use. For example, researchers at the National Center on Addiction and Substance Abuse at

MOTHERS AGAINST DRUNK DRIVING (MADD)

In 1980, Californian Candace Lightner, whose daughter was killed by a drunk driver, founded Mothers Against Drunk Driving (MADD). According to the organization's website, MADD's mission is to stop drunk driving, fight against drugged driving, support those who have been affected by drunk driving, and stop underage drinking. Their Campaign to Eliminate Drunk Driving has three aims:

1. To support law enforcement working in the field to end drunk driving.

2. To demand that drunk drivers have breathalyzer devices in their cars that would prevent the cars from starting if the driver was inebriated.

3. To advocate for new technology that would automatically determine a driver's blood alcohol concentration (BAC) before the driver attempted to start his vehicle. This technology would keep the car from starting if the driver's BAC was above the legal limit of 0.08.

MADD has many resources for those fighting against underage drinking as part of their Power of You(th) and Power of Parents campaign. These resources include handbooks for parents, educators, community leaders, and teens. The teen handbook provides young people with facts on the damage that alcohol can do to their bodies, brains, and reputation and encourages teens to talk openly with their parents about alcohol use and abuse. There is also a section devoted to how to help a friend whose drinking concerns you, including tips on how to approach her with your concerns.

Columbia University (CASA) found that 29 percent of teens were left home unsupervised overnight, and those teens were twice as likely to have used alcohol as their peers who were not left alone. Along with this finding, the researchers determined that teens who say their parents don't have a problem with teenage drinking were ten times more likely to say that it was OK for kids their age to get drunk.

How parents act matters, too. If the first thing a teen's mother or father does at the end of a long workday is pour a scotch or pop open a beer that sends a message that drinking is a good way to release tension and reward yourself. Maybe wine is always served at dinner and the kids in the household have been allowed to take a few sips now and then. This lax attitude can leave a lasting impression as children grow older and face making choices about whether or not to use alcohol.

A parent can be a positive influence, too. Sitting down for a family dinner, helping with homework, or otherwise spending quality time with a teen can help him or her stay

If a parent drinks to deal with stress, her children may get the message that alcohol is a good way to cope when life gets difficult.

away from alcohol. A series of studies by CASA determined that teens who don't have family dinners five to seven nights a week are twice as likely to have used alcohol.

MEDIA MESSAGES

When the Denver Broncos won Super Bowl 50 on February 7, 2016, quarterback Peyton Manning told a reporter from CBS Sports that he was going to drink a lot of Budweiser beer to celebrate the win. To have the Super Bowl's winning quarterback equate beer with good times sends a strong message, especially to those who are young and impressionable. Young people are also exposed to many advertisements for alcohol, as manufacturers spend billions of dollars in advertising on television and other media.

All this alcohol promotion seems to be having an effect. A 2013 study by the School of Community and Global Health at Claremont College found that seventh grade students who stated that they enjoyed the television ads they saw were more likely to have problems with alcohol, particularly boys.

Social media has a significant impact on teens, too. According to a 2012 study by CASA, 75 percent of twelve- to seventeen-year-olds who saw pictures of teens using alcohol or marijuana on social media sites wanted to "party like that." In addition, when compared to teens who never saw pictures of someone drunk, passed out, or using drugs on social media, those that have seen such activity were more than three times more likely to have used alcohol.

DRINKING PROBLEMS

Alcohol use is defined as drinking alcohol on occasion and not to excess. If someone's drinking has had a negative effect on his life, he is said to have an alcohol use disorder (AUD). *The Diagnostic and Statistical Manual*, 5th edition (*DSM-5*), which classifies mental disorders, lists symptoms for an AUD. How many symptoms apply to a person determines whether he has a mild, moderate, or severe disorder.

There are a series of questions that a psychiatrist, psychologist, or addiction medicine specialist will ask a client to find out if he has an AUD. The *DSM-5* has one screening tool used by many in the field, while the Alcohol

If a teen abuses alcohol, she may no longer care about her appearance or how others perceive her. Getting her next drink is more important than her reputation.

Use Disorders Identification Test (AUDIT) is another tool that is commonly used. These questionnaires cover topics such as how much time a person spends drinking, whether his drinking has led to trouble at home or at work, whether he has tried to stop drinking, and whether he feels guilty about his drinking.

If your friend is abusing alcohol he may start acting differently. He may get bad grades or skip school altogether. He may start hanging out with a different group of friends or withdraw from people completely. His appearance may suffer, as he no longer cares about looking attractive. Lack of interest in everyday activities is a warning sign of a drinking problem, as is low energy.

A DREADED DISEASE

Heavy drinkers can become physically dependent on alcohol. This dependency is what people commonly think of when they think of alcoholism. Those with a severe AUD crave alcohol and are not able to stop drinking or even to cut back on the amount they drink. They keep drinking even though it makes them sick and is destroying their lives. They can't just "snap out of it" and stop drinking, for their need for alcohol is like someone else's need for water. They are addicted.

A teen with an alcohol use disorder continues to drink even though it is making him physically ill. His craving for alcohol is stronger than any desire to stop drinking.

Alcoholism is a chronic disease that can affect any age, but according to the National Institute on Alcohol Abuse and Alcoholism (NIAAA) teens that start drinking before age fifteen are four times more likely to develop alcohol dependence at some point. Children of alcoholics are four times more likely to have problems with alcohol. This vulnerability is partly genetic, but is also influenced by the environment in which the teen grows up and how his parents act around him and each other. People with mental illness and those who were abused as children also have a greater chance of developing an alcohol use disorder.

MYTHS AND FACTS

MYTH: It's OK to drive if you've had only a drink or two.

FACT: Even one or two drinks can prevent you from driving safely. So-called buzzed driving is drunk driving.

MYTH: It's better to drink than take drugs.

FACT: Alcohol *is* a drug and one that can cause great damage to your brain and body.

MYTH: It's safer to drink beer than wine or hard liquor.

FACT: A can of beer has as much alcohol as a glass of wine or a shot of liquor so it's no safer to drink beer.

CHAPTER THREE

A FRIEND IN NEED

If you believe your friend has an alcohol problem, you may wonder if it's your place to get involved. Maybe you feel like it's none of your business, but think of it this way: If your friend were choking and you knew the Heimlich maneuver, you'd spring into action, right? Even if you couldn't help him yourself, you'd find someone who could. Well an alcohol use disorder calls for an equally urgent response. Your friend might drink and drive and get into an accident. He might get involved in a sexual situation that leads to physical or emotional harm. Binge drinking could result in your friend suffering from alcohol poisoning.

Perhaps you're worried about going it alone, but you should never try to handle your friend's alcohol problem on your own. You can approach him with your concerns and offer support and advice, but he needs medical and therapeutic professionals to help him deal with his issues. You need support, too, and can find help from a parent, guidance counselor, coach, or another trusted adult. If your biggest fear is that you'll get your friend in trouble, take this advice from MADD's *Teen Handbook*: "Don't worry

When talking to a friend with an alcohol problem, focus on his behavior, not his character. Be specific about your concerns, and let him know you're there to help.

that you'll get your friend in trouble. Your friend is already in trouble."

STARTING THE CONVERSATION

When you're ready to approach your friend about her alcohol problem, there are several things to keep in mind. It is important to make sure that your friend is sober when you talk and that the two of you are in a quiet place where you won't be interrupted.

During your conversation, be as specific as possible. Don't just say "you drink too much," but something along the lines of "I noticed that you were downing a lot of beers the other night. I was really worried that you were going to get sick." Using statements that start with "I" are much less threatening than "you" statements, which can come across as blaming the person with the problem. Along the same lines, make sure to challenge your friend's behavior, not her character. You can say that it really hurts you to see your friend acting in an unsafe way, but never call her a loser or say that she simply needs to pull herself together.

You can also talk to your friend about some of the possible underlying reasons for his or her drinking. Saying "I know you've been stressed lately because your folks are divorcing" or "I know your breakup was hard on you" is a great way to show that you understand what she is going through and want to be there to support her.

LOOKING FOR GUIDANCE

If your friend agrees that he has a problem and is willing to get help, you can go with him to talk with a trusted adult. It may be less frightening to speak with a teacher or guidance counselor rather than a parent, but know that the teacher or counselor will likely contact your friend's parents as they need to be involved in any further discussions. You might think that your friend's parents are already aware of the problem, but they may be in denial about what seems obvious to you. Going with your friend to talk to a parent is another great way to be supportive. This discussion will likely be a tough conversation to have, but if your friend is going to deal head on with his alcohol problem, his parents need to be part of the process.

If your friend is willing to get help for her alcohol use disorder, it's important that her parents be involved every step of the way.

Your friend's next best step is going to a doctor with a background in addiction medicine. She will ask your friend questions about whether he's driven a car after using alcohol or been a passenger in a car with someone who was drunk. She'll want to know if your friend uses alcohol to relax, whether he drinks alone, and if he's ever had memory lapses after drinking.

If a doctor who is certified in addiction medicine is not available, a general pediatrician or adolescent medicine specialist can steer your friend toward the help he needs. A great place to start is the Substance Abuse and Mental Health Service's Administration (SAMHSA) national helpline at 1-800-662-HELP. SAMHSA's treatment locator (www.findtreatment.samhsa.gov) will help him find the care he needs as he deals with his alcohol problem.

A popular support for those with AUDs is Alcoholics Anonymous (AA), which holds meetings to aid those trying to recover from addiction. You can offer to attend a meeting with your friend if he's nervous about going alone. There are also Alateen meetings, which are intended for teenage friends and family members of those

ALATEEN

Alateen is a support and fellowship group for young people whose lives have been affected by a friend or family member's alcohol problem. During Alateen meetings, group members recount their experiences in the hope that what is shared will help another teen cope with someone else's AUD. Alateen, which is part of the Al-Anon Family Group, stresses the fact that alcoholism is a disease. The members of Alateen are encouraged to remember that they are not the reason someone drinks and that they can't control another person's actions. One aim of Alateen is to have the friend or relative maintain strict boundaries with the person with the alcohol problem to avoid becoming emotionally overwhelmed. The Al-Anon/Alateen website offers first-person accounts of teens dealing with someone else's drinking problem as well as an online chat room for young people confronting these issues.

struggling with addiction. You are not obligated to attend these meetings for any set amount of time so you might want to check one out to see if it suits you.

A BAD RESPONSE

What do you do if your friend is unwilling to get help? Given that you've brought up a sore subject, there's a chance she won't respond in a positive way. She may deny that there's anything wrong or tell you to butt out of other people's business. She may become angry or walk away. Although this outcome is disappointing, you shouldn't blame either your friend or yourself. At least you've shown

Your friend may become angry or defensive when approached about his alcohol problem. Although you may feel hurt by this response, at least you've shown that you care.

your friend that you're aware of the problem and care about her.

You may feel the need to set boundaries with your friend. You can tell her that you're not going to hang out with her when she's drunk or offer excuses for her behavior to her other friends and family. Maybe you will no longer give her the notes for class when she's skipped again because she has a hangover. You shouldn't take these measures to punish your friend, but to protect yourself and to let her know how seriously you take her issues with alcohol.

After you've spoken with your friend directly, find an adult to talk to about your feelings regarding your friend's alcohol use. They can help you work through the fear, confusion, anger, and other emotions that the situation brings out in you. If you're talking to your parents, don't expect them to keep what you've told them secret. Your friend's well-being—or even her life—is on the line and your parents will likely feel the need to let her parents know what is happening.

SETTING THE STAGE

If your friend continues to refuse to get help, family, friends, and other loved ones might stage what is known as an intervention. During an intervention, the important people in your friend's life will state their concerns

During an intervention, friends and family members tell the person with the alcohol problem how his or her drinking has negatively impacted their lives.

about his drinking and let him know how his actions have affected them. They might read from letters they've written detailing the ways in which your friend's drinking has impacted the relationship. These impact letters—and every part of the intervention—must stress that your friend is loved and that no one is blaming him for his condition. An impact letter often ends with specifics about treatment programs available to your friend, so the group should make sure they've done their research ahead of time and have resources at hand.

A trained therapist or substance abuse counselor may be part of an intervention. These interventionists run the meeting and keep things from getting too heated, as emotions will no doubt be running high. There is no room for anger in an intervention as this is likely to make your friend even more resistant to change.

You shouldn't feel compelled to take part in an intervention. It is an intense process, and you and your parents may decide it's best for you to stay on the sidelines. If you do take part, know that you hold no responsibility for the outcome. Your friend may still refuse help, and it is up to his parents to decide the next step. In many states it is legal for parents to place their child in treatment without his consent if he is under eighteen. Of course the hope is that he will enter treatment willingly as this will be much less traumatic for all concerned.

TAKING CARE

Dealing with a friend with an alcohol problem is a very stressful situation. Although it's great that you're invested in your friendship, you can't forget to take care of yourself, as well. It's important to continue to talk with a therapist, guidance counselor, or another trusted adult about the feelings your friend's drinking is bringing up. It might be helpful to keep a journal, because writing about your experience can help release negative feelings that are bottling up inside.

Make sure to get enough exercise, whether that's as part of a team or on your own, because keeping active is a great stress reliever. Eating well is vital for your overall health, so avoid junk food in favor of fruits, vegetables, and protein. As a good night's sleep can do wonders for your mood and energy level, try to get your full eight to nine hours.

You might want to take a look at your own drinking habits, too. Hopefully you don't drink at all, but if you do and want to cut down—or preferably stop—there are actions you can take. If you find yourself thinking about drinking, find a new activity to keep your mind and body busy. Join a club or try out for a sport that's always interested you. Avoid what the NIAAA's *Rethinking Drinking* refers to as "triggers," which are events or people that give you the urge to drink. When you're unable to avoid those triggers, remember the reasons you wanted to cut back on your drinking or speak with someone you know will support what you're trying to do. Knowing you can get through those urges will make you feel all that much stronger.

10 GREAT QUESTIONS TO ASK A GUIDANCE COUNSELOR

1 HOW CAN I BE SURE MY FRIEND HAS AN ALCOHOL PROBLEM?

2 HOW CAN I HELP MY FRIEND WITHOUT GETTING HIM IN TROUBLE?

3 WHAT DO I DO WHEN MY FRIEND ASKS ME TO COVER FOR HIM BECAUSE HE'S TOO HUNG OVER TO MAKE IT TO SCHOOL?

4 IF MY FRIEND SEEMS DEPRESSED COULD THAT HAVE SOMETHING TO DO WITH HIS DRINKING?

5 SHOULD I TELL MY FRIEND'S PARENTS ABOUT HIS ALCOHOL PROBLEM BEFORE I SPEAK TO HIM?

6 WHAT DO I DO IF MY FRIEND DENIES HE HAS AN ALCOHOL PROBLEM?

7 HOW CAN I KEEP MY FRIEND'S ALCOHOL PROBLEM FROM STRESSING ME OUT?

8 WHAT IS THE BEST TREATMENT FOR AN ALCOHOL USE DISORDER?

9 WHAT CAN I DO TO SUPPORT MY FRIEND DURING HIS RECOVERY FROM HIS ALCOHOL PROBLEM?

10 CAN PEOPLE WITH ALCOHOL USE DISORDERS EVER DRINK AGAIN?

CHAPTER FOUR

THE BEST TREATMENT

When your friend is ready for treatment for her alcohol problem, there are several options available to her, depending on her needs. Although the thought of dealing with her AUD might seem overwhelming, most people do well with some type of treatment. According to the NIAAA, approximately one-third of people who get treated for an AUD are symptom free a year later. Many more have cut down on their drinking to the point where they report fewer problems related to their AUD.

Keeping in mind that each case is different, the National Institute on Drug Abuse states that successful treatment requires several key steps. These include the following:

- Detoxification
- Behavioral counseling
- Medications
- Evaluation and treatment of mental health issues
- Long-term follow-up to avoid drinking alcohol again, which is called relapse

Recovering from an alcohol problem takes a strong commitment and it is not an easy path to follow. You can support your friend by being a sounding board and letting her know that you are rooting for her to get healthy.

THE RIGHT WAY TO GO

After someone has been drinking heavily for weeks, months, or years, his nervous system gets used to being alcohol fueled. If that alcohol is taken away, as David Sheff puts it in *Clean: Overcoming Addiction and Ending*

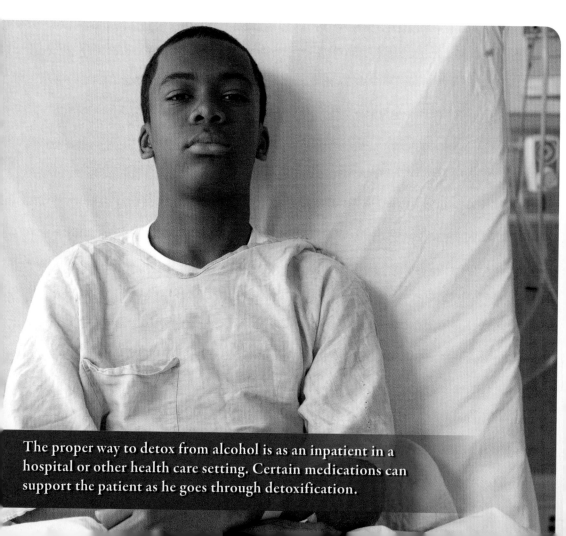

The proper way to detox from alcohol is as an inpatient in a hospital or other health care setting. Certain medications can support the patient as he goes through detoxification.

America's Greatest Tragedy "cells are dying and neurons misfiring," which can lead to symptoms such as anxiety, nausea, seizures, and even hallucinations. For heavy long-term users withdrawing from alcohol, the delirium tremens (DTs) can result in shaking, sweating, an irregular heartbeat, and severe mental confusion. The fact that the DTs are also called "the horrors" shows just how difficult they are to handle.

Detoxification (detox) is the process by which a person with an AUD rids his body of alcohol. If detox is necessary it should not be attempted alone. The suggestion that someone can grit his teeth and power through detox without medical help is not only misguided, but also potentially dangerous. David Sheff believes that this attitude stems from the idea that those with drinking problems need to be punished for their bad behavior rather than treated as people who are sick.

Medical detox, which is usually done in a hospital or other inpatient health care facility, begins with a medical exam and patient history. Drug testing is done to confirm the presence of alcohol in the person's system and to see if he has taken other drugs, as well.

Medications are a part of medical detox. Drugs such as diazepam (Valium), lorazepam (Ativan), and chlordiazepoxide (Librium) are used to support someone as he transitions through withdrawal. These drugs are from a class of medications called benzodiazepines, which can lessen anxiety, aid sleep, and prevent seizures as he begins to detox. Drugs known as atypical antipsychotics are also used during detox to lessen anxiety and depression.

MAKING A CHOICE

The first choice your friend and her family will have to make is whether she will receive treatment on an inpatient or outpatient basis. That choice will depend on the severity of her illness, what works best for her family, and perhaps cost, as inpatient stays are expensive and not always covered by health insurance. Another option is to begin treatment with an inpatient stay followed by longer-term outpatient care.

Residential treatment facilities are very structured and offer intensive services, including medical care. In what is called a therapeutic community, patients stay at the residence for up to a year. The staff and fellow patients will try to influence your friend in a positive way as she seeks to change the thoughts and behaviors that led to her alcohol problem. Shorter-term residential treatment is also available. This type of treatment is often used for detoxification and for intensive therapy to get someone ready to be treated on an outpatient basis. There is also short-term housing for those leaving inpatient treatment. This recovery housing helps patients transition back to their everyday lives and connects them with resources in their community.

Whether inpatient or outpatient, it is vital that the program be the right match for your friend. When evaluating where to get treatment, she should find out what approach the program takes, whether that program will be tailored to her needs, what will be expected of her as a patient, and how those in charge measure success. As your friend and her family make their decision, it is important to zone in on a program that makes her feel heard and respected.

LEARNING TO COPE

It's important to make sure that a treatment program matches the patient's needs. To find the right fit, check what activities the program offers and what is expected of patients.

Some type of behavioral counseling is common to most treatment programs. Behavioral counseling helps someone with an AUD gain the skills to stop drinking and to deal with those triggers that may make him want to drink. A psychologist, psychiatrist, or licensed substance abuse counselor will help him work toward his treatment goals and build up a support system to see him through this trying time.

There are various behavioral treatments tailored toward those with AUDs. In cognitive-behavioral therapy, which can be done one-on-one or in a group, the aim is to recognize the feelings and situations that cause the person to drink heavily and think about new ways to cope with those feelings without turning to alcohol.

While recovering from an alcohol problem, your friend should steer clear of events where people will be drinking. Watching a movie or playing a sport is a much better option.

Motivational enhancement therapy (MET) is short term and meant to increase the person's desire to get better. The patient and his counselor discuss the pros and cons of treatment and design a plan to help him change his drinking behavior. MET also aims to build up the person's confidence and work on skills that will allow him to be successful with his stated goals.

Another important component to treatment is family counseling, which brings close relatives into the therapeutic process. The goal of family therapy is to deal with underlying issues that may influence your friend's drinking and to strengthen the bonds between family members. In doing so, the family can support their loved one as he works toward a sober lifestyle.

Medications to deal with alcohol addiction (as opposed to those used for detox) are also available in both an inpatient and outpatient setting. Disulfiram (Antabuse) makes someone "allergic" to alcohol, in the sense that if he drinks any alcohol while on the drug he will have symptoms such as nausea, headache, and heart palpitations. According to Robert Doyle and Joseph Nowinski, authors of *Almost Alcoholic*, Antabuse can reduce how often an addicted person drinks by as much as 50 percent. The drug naltrexone works not by making one sick, but by taking away the pleasurable sensations that can come from drinking alcohol and lessening the craving for the drug. Acamprosate (Campral) helps reduce the symptoms of withdrawal such as anxiety, restlessness, and trouble falling asleep or staying asleep. All of these medications must be taken under close medical supervision.

MENTAL HEALTH DISORDERS

When your friend first begins treatment for her AUD, she will also be screened to determine whether she also has an underlying mental illness, also known as a mental health disorder. A mental illness is more than feeling stressed-out or sad occasionally. Someone with a mental health disorder has extreme feelings that she finds hard to manage or may experience a lack of feeling or expression that is worrisome. Those with mental illness may have moods that make it tough to be around them, but they are not trying to be challenging. They are ill and need quality treatment to live a more fulfilling life.

If your friend has a mental illness as well as an alcohol use disorder, he will have a treatment team to help him deal with both issues.

Some of the more common mental health disorders that teens suffer from include anxiety disorder, depression, attention deficit hyperactivity disorder (ADHD), and bipolar disorder. Bipolar disorder causes severe mood swings between depression and mania, a state where one feels either joyous and full of energy or extremely irritable.

When a person has both a mental illness and an AUD, she is said to have a dual diagnosis. The relationship between mental illness and an alcohol problem is a complicated one because mental illness can lead someone to self-medicate with alcohol, and an AUD can worsen the symptoms of a mental illness.

STUDENTS AGAINST DESTRUCTIVE DECISIONS (SADD)

The mission of Students Against Destructive Decisions (SADD), according to SADD's website, is to "empower young people to successfully confront the risks and pressures that challenge them in their daily lives." SADD, a national organization, advocates peer-to-peer education with teachers and counselors advising groups that are led by students. These groups seek to help teens deal with issues including traffic safety, personal health and safety, and drug and alcohol abuse. One way SADD fights against substance abuse is by staging so-called reality parties for parents of teens. At a reality party, students from a local SADD chapter act out what might happen at a party at a teen's home. During this fictional party, parents take a tour through a house and see scenes of drinking games, fighting, dating violence, and peer pressure play out. In one reality party in Lima, Ohio, the mother of the teen hosting the party is shown being led away in handcuffs after one of the partygoers at her house is knocked unconscious. The event is meant to educate parents about what might go on at a party and to underscore their moral and legal responsibility when it comes to teen drinking. As Kelly Pritchard, the student adviser for SADD told a reporter from the *Lima News* "I want parents to learn what teenagers need from parents to help them make the right decisions."

If your friend has a dual diagnosis, she needs help with both conditions. All members of her treatment team must communicate with each other to make sure she is receiving targeted therapy. It is likely that a psychiatrist will prescribe medications for her mental illness. Those medications must be monitored to watch for side effects and for any interaction with other drugs she might be taking for an AUD.

THE ROAD TO RECOVERY

It is common for those in recovery from alcoholism to attend AA meetings on a regular basis. According to Dr. Steven

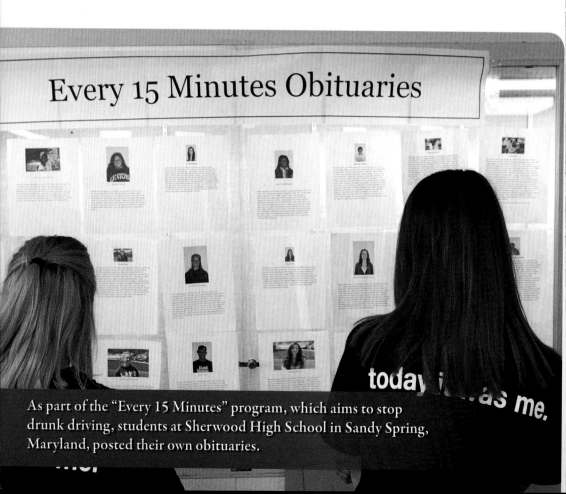

As part of the "Every 15 Minutes" program, which aims to stop drunk driving, students at Sherwood High School in Sandy Spring, Maryland, posted their own obituaries.

Jaffe, a psychiatrist who spoke about these issues at a 2012 American Society of Addiction Medicine conference, teens have tremendous anxiety about going to AA. Dr. Jaffe also said teens should be accompanied by someone farther along in his recovery—known as a sponsor—to support them.

There are also parts of the program that may need to be adapted for teens. One of the core concepts of AA is that people are powerless over alcohol, and teens will be turned off by the idea of giving up their power. Instead, Dr. Jaffe recommends that teens be told that getting sober will strengthen their power. Another concept of AA that may be difficult for teens is that of surrender, as many teens have found themselves in vulnerable positions because of their drinking. "I tell them if they get clean and sober, they'll be strong, and never have to put themselves in a position where bad things like that can happen," Dr. Jaffe states.

Along with accompanying your friend to an AA meeting, you can support him by serving as a positive example. Not only can you get your own drinking in check, but you can also can plan events that do not revolve around alcohol. Skip that party and go to a movie or do something active like going for a run or playing basketball. Encourage him to take up a new hobby or to reconnect with friends who are not part of the partying scene. Perhaps both of you join your local SADD chapter—or help start one if none exists. While you're taking all these steps to help your friend, don't forget to pay attention to your own needs. You can be a great friend and still keep some distance to avoid getting overwhelmed by his alcohol problem. Then you can be there for him in a healthy way as he continues down the road to recovery.

GLOSSARY

ADDICTED Physically and psychologically dependent to the point where a person is unable to stop engaging in the activity despite its negative effects on his health and well-being.

ATTENTION DEFICIT HYPERACTIVITY DISORDER (ADHD) A mental health disorder that affects a person's ability to pay attention and process information. Those with ADHD can also have difficulty keeping their body still and may act in an impulsive manner.

CENTRAL NERVOUS SYSTEM A complex network of tissue that controls the body and the mind. It includes the brain and the spinal cord.

CHRONIC Having an illness that lasts for a long time or keeps coming back.

CIRRHOSIS A chronic disease whereby toxins released by the breaking down of alcohol cause damage to cells in the liver.

COGNITIVE Having to do with thinking, learning, understanding, and memory.

COMMUNITY SERVICE Work performed by a person or a group of people to help an organization or community. Someone who has been arrested can be required to perform community service instead of, or in addition to, spending time in jail.

CONSCIOUSNESS The state of being awake and fully aware of what is going on around you.

DEFICIT Not having enough of something that is required.

DEHYDRATION To lose so much liquid in the body that it becomes harmful. Symptoms of dehydration include dizziness, headaches, and overall weakness.

DEPTH PERCEPTION The way two eyes work together to see objects in three dimensions. Depth perception helps determine both how large and how far away an object is.

ENDORPHINS Neurotransmitters that block pain signals and cause a heightened sense of pleasure.

FAMILY COUNSELING A type of counseling meant to strengthen relationships among family members by improving communication and working through conflicts.

GENETIC Characteristics inherited from one generation to another.

INEBRIATED Negatively impacted by alcohol to a degree that physical and mental processes are affected.

INTERVENTION A meeting during which friends and family members urge someone to get help for his alcohol addiction.

PREFRONTAL CORTEX The part of the brain located just behind the forehead. It controls social behavior and decision making.

RECOVERY The process by which an addicted person does not drink alcohol to lead a healthier and more productive life.

SEIZURES Sudden uncontrollable movements of the body caused by illness or by ingesting a toxic substance.

SELF-MEDICATE To take drugs without a doctor's supervision to deal with difficult emotions such as anxiety or depression.

SEXUAL ASSAULT An attack that involves forced sexual contact without the other person's consent.

THERAPEUTIC COMMUNITY An intensive inpatient treatment program for those with alcohol use disorders and substance use disorders.

FOR MORE INFORMATION

Al-Anon/Alateen Family Group Headquarters, Inc.
1600 Corporate Landing Parkway
Virginia Beach, VA 23454-5617
(888) 4AL-ANON
Website: http://www.al-anon.alateen.org
Al-Anon/Alateen meetings provide mutual support for friends
and family members of people with alcohol problems.

Alcoholics Anonymous (AA)
AA World Services, Inc.
PO Box 459
Grand Central Station
New York, NY 10163
(212) 870-3400
Website: http://www.aa.org
Alcoholics Anonymous offers support and fellowship to those
dealing with an alcohol use disorder (AUD). AA meetings are
held throughout the world.

Canadian Centre on Substance Abuse
75 Albert Street, Suite 500
Ottawa, ON K1P 5E7
Canada
(613) 235-4048
Website: http://www.ccsa.ca
The Canadian Centre on Substance Abuse aims to increase
awareness of substance abuse issues, reduce the harm
caused by alcohol use, and address the problem of fetal alcohol syndrome.

Center for Substance Abuse Treatment
Substance Abuse and Mental Health Services Administration
  (SAMHSA)
1 Choke Cherry Road
Rockville, MD 20857
(240) 276-1660
Website: http://www.samhsa.gov/about/csat.aspx
SAMHSA's resources include a twenty-four-hour national
  helpline [(800) 662-HELP (4357)] to support those in need of
  services for their alcohol problem or mental health disorder.
  SAMHSA is an agency within the U.S. Department of Health
  and Human Services.

Centre for Addiction and Mental Health
33 Russell Street
Toronto, ON M5S 2S1
Canada
(800) 463-6273
Website: http://www.camh.net
The focus of the Centre for Addiction and Mental Health is
  providing education and treatment for those with addiction
  and mental health issues.

Health Canada
Address Locator 0900C2
Ottawa, ON K1A 0K9
Canada
(866) 225-0709
Website: http://www.hc-sc.gc.ca
Health Canada publishes information on preventing substance
  use problems among teens, how to talk to teens about drugs,
  and best treatment practices for those dealing with a sub-
  stance use disorder, among other topics.

Mothers Against Drunk Driving (MADD)
National Office
511 East John Freeway
Suite 700
Irving, TX 75062
(877) ASK-MADD
Website: http://www.madd.org
Mother's Against Drunk Driving is dedicated to stopping
drunk and drugged driving, helping those victimized by these
crimes, and preventing underage drinking.

Students Against Destructive Decisions (SADD)
255 Main Street
Marlborough, MA 01752
(877) SADD-INC
Website: http://www.sadd.org
Students Against Destructive Decisions empowers teens to
address issues such as substance abuse, traffic safety, bullying, and teen violence.

WEBSITES

Because of the changing nature of internet links, Rosen Publishing has developed an online list of websites related to the
subject of this book. This site is updated regularly. Please use
this link to access the list:

http://www.rosenlinks.com/HCIH/alcohol

FOR FURTHER READING

Ambrose, Marylou. *Investigate Alcohol* (Investigate Drugs). New York, NY: Enslow Publishing, 2014.

Bjonlund, Lydia. *Alcohol* (21st Century Skills Library: Health at Risk). North Mankato, MN: Cherry Lake Publishing, 2008.

Brezina, Carona. *Alcohol and Drug Offenses: Your Legal Rights* (Know Your Rights). New York, NY: Rosen Publishing, 2015.

Brezina, Corona. *I've Gotten a DWI/DUI. Now What?* (Teen Life 411). New York, NY: Rosen Publishing, 2016.

Espejo, Roman. *Alcohol* (Teen Rights and Freedoms). Farmington Hills, MI: Greenhaven Press, 2012.

Henneberg, Susan. *Defeating Addiction and Alcoholism* (Effective Survival Strategies). New York, NY: Rosen Publishing, 2016.

Levete, Sarah. *The Hidden Story of Alcoholism* (Undercover Story). New York, NY: Rosen Publishing, 2014.

Lily, Henrietta M., and Daniel E. Harmon. *Frequently Asked Questions About Alcohol Abuse and Binge Drinking* (FAQ: Teen Life). New York, NY: Rosen Publishing, 2012.

Mendralla, Valerie, and Janet Grosshandler. *Drinking and Driving. Now What?* (Teen Life 411). New York, NY: Rosen Publishing, 2012.

Meyer, Terry Teague. *I Have an Alcoholic Parent. Now What?* (Teen Life 411). New York, NY: Rosen Publishing, 2015.

Mooney, Al J., Howard Eisenberg, and Catherine Dold. *The Recovery Book: Answers to All Your Questions About Addiction and Alcoholism and Finding Health and Happiness in Sobriety.* New York, NY: Workman Publishing, 2014.

Radev, Anna, ed. *I've Got This Friend Who...Advice for Teens and Their Friends on Alcohol, Drugs, Eating Disorders, Risky Behavior, and More.* Center City, MN: Hazelden, 2012.

Rogers, Kara, ed. *Substance Use and Abuse* (Health and Disease in Society). New York, NY: Britannica Educational Publishing, 2011.

Saltzman, Amy. *A Still Quiet Place for Teens: A Mindfulness Workbook to Ease Stress and Difficult Emotions* (An Instant Help Book for Teens). Oakland, CA: New Harbinger Publications, 2016.

Sheff, David. *Beautiful Boy: A Father's Journey Through His Son's Addiction*. New York, NY: Houghton Mifflin Company, 2008.

Sheff, Nic. *We All Fall Down: Living with Addiction*. New York, NY: Little Brown, 2012.

Skeen, Michelle, Matthew McKay, Patrick Fanning, and Kelly Skeen. *Communication Skills for Teens: How to Listen, Express, and Connect for Success* (The Instant Help Solutions Series). Oakland, CA: New Harbinger Publications, 2016.

Snyder, Gail. *Teens and Alcohol* (Gallup Youth Survey: Major Issues and Trends). Broomall, PA: Mason Crest Publishers, 2013.

Thayne, Tim. *Not By Chance: How Parents Boost Their Teen's Success In and After Treatment*. Charleston, SC: Advantage Media Group, 2013.

Van Dijk, Sheri. *Relationship Skills 101 for Teens: Your Guide to Dealing with Daily Drama, Stress, and Difficult Emotions using DBT* (The Instant Help Solutions Series). Oakland, CA: New Harbinger Publications, 2015.

Williams, Rebecca E., and Julie S. Kraft. *The Mindfulness Workbook for Addiction: A Guide to Coping with the Grief, Stress, and Anger that Trigger Addictive Behaviors*. Oakland, CA: New Harbinger Publications, 2012.

BIBLIOGRAPHY

Bellenir, Karen, ed. *Alcohol Information for Teens.* 3rd ed. Detroit, MI: Omnigraphics, 2013.

Centers for Disease Control and Prevention. "Fact Sheet: Caffeine and Alcohol." Retrieved February 10, 2010 (http://www.cdc.gov/alcohol/fact-sheets/caffeine-and-alcohol.htm).

Currie-McGhee, Leanne K. *Teenage Alcoholism* (Compact Research). San Diego, CA: ReferencePoint Press, 2012.

Doyle, Robert, and Joseph Nowinski. *Almost Alcoholic: Is My (or My Loved One's) Drinking a Problem.* Center City, MN: Hazelden, 2012.

Mothers Against Drunk Driving (MADD). "Campaign to Eliminate Drunk Driving." Retrieved February 27, 2016 (http://www.madd.org/drunk-driving/campaign/).

Mothers Against Drunk Driving (MADD). *Teen Handbook.* Retrieved February 27, 2016 (http://www.madd.org/underage-drinking/power-of-youth/get-the-power-of-youth-teen.html).

National Alliance on Mental Illness. "Fact Sheet: Dual Diagnosis." Retrieved February 20, 2016 (http://www.nami.org/Learn-More/Mental-Health-Conditions/Related-Conditions/Dual-Diagnosis).

The National Center on Addiction and Substance Abuse at Columbia University. *The Importance of Family Dinners VIII.* September 2012 (http://www.centeronaddiction.org/addiction-research/reports/importance-of-family-dinners-2012).

The National Center on Addiction and Substance Abuse at Columbia University. *National Survey of American Attitudes on Substance Abuse XVII: Teens.* August 2012. (http://www.centeronaddiction.org/addiction-research/reports/national-survey-american-attitudes-substance-abuse-teens-2012)

National Institute on Alcohol Abuse and Alcoholism. "Fact Sheet: College Drinking." Retrieved February 25, 2016 (http://niaaa.nih.gov/alcohol-health/special-populations-co-occurring-disorders/college-drinking).

National Institute on Alcohol Abuse and Alcoholism. "Fact Sheet: Underage Drinking." Retrieved February 10, 2016 (http://niaaa.nih.gov/alcohol-health/special-populations-co-occurring-disorders/underage-drinking).

National Institute on Alcohol Abuse and Alcoholism. *Rethinking Drinking.* December 2015 (http://rethinkingdrinking.niaaa.nih.gov).

National Institute on Alcohol Abuse and Alcoholism. *Treatment for Alcohol Problems: Finding and Getting Help.* Retrieved March 4, 2016 (http://pubs.niaaa.nih.gov/publications/treatment/treatment.htm).

National Institute on Drug Abuse. *Treatment Approaches for Drug Addiction.* January 2016 (https://www.drugabuse.gov/publications/drugfacts/treatment-approaches-drug-addiction).

Partnership for Drug-Free Kids. *What to Do if Your Child Is Drinking or Using Drugs.* Retrieved February 15, 2016 (http://www.drugfree.org/resources/intervention-e-book-what-to-do-if-your-child-is-drinking-or-using-drugs/).

Science Daily. "Teens Who Drink Alone More Likely to Develop Alcohol Problems as Young Adults." November 18, 2013 (https://www.sciencedaily.com/releases/2013/11/131118103937.htm).

Sheff, David. *Clean: Overcoming Addiction and Ending America's Greatest Tragedy.* New York, NY: Houghton Mifflin Harcourt, 2013.

Sowinski, Greg. "SADD Students Educate Parents on Dangers of Parties, Alcohol." *Lima News,* February 15, 2016 (http://limaohio.com/news/166511/sadd-students-educate-parents-on-dangers-of-parties-alcohol).

Stewart, Gail B. *Teens and Drinking* (Teen Choices). San Diego, CA: ReferencePoint Press, 2016.

Substance Abuse and Mental Health Services Administration. *Behavioral Health Trends in the United States: Results from the 2014 Survey on Drug Use and Health.* September 2015 (http://www.samhsa.gov).

Trudeau, Michelle. "Teen Drinking May Cause Irreversible Brain Damage." *National Public Radio's Morning Edition,* January 25, 2010 (http://www.npr.org/templates/story/story .php?storyId=122765890).

Vimont, Celia. "Adapting 12-Step Programs for Teenagers." Partnership for Drug-Free Kids. June 1, 2012 (http://www .drugfree.org/join-together/adapting-12-step-programs-for-teenagers/).

INDEX

ABOUT THE AUTHOR

Jennifer Landau received her MA degree in creative writing from New York University and her MST in general and special education from Fordham University. She is an experienced editor and has written several titles for young adults, including *How to Beat Psychological Bullying, Dealing with Bullies, Cliques, and Social Stress*, and *Bipolar Disorder*. When she is not writing, she enjoys reading across all genres and spending time outdoors with her son.

PHOTO CREDITS

Cover © iStockphoto.com/Katarzyna Bialasiewicz; p. 5 Peter Dazeley/Photographer's Choice/Getty Images; p. 10 Image Source/Getty Images; p. 11 Jim Varney/Science Source; p. 14 Pascal Goetgheluck/Science Source; p. 17 Science Picture Co./Collection Mix Subjects/Getty Images; p. 20 Cultura RM Exclusive/Seb Oliver/Getty Images; p. 24 Photofusion/Universal Images Group/Getty Images; p. 26 sturti/E+/Getty Images; p. 27 PYMCA/Universal Images Group/Getty Images; p. 31 Huy Lam/First Light/Getty Images; p. 33 Bruce Ayres/The Image Bank/Getty Images; p. 35 Hill Street Studios/Gary Kious/Blend Images/Getty Images; pp. 36–37 Altrendo images/Getty Images; p. 42 ERproductions Ltd/Blend Images/Getty Images; p. 45 Guang Niu/Photolibrary/Getty Images; p. 46 Peter Cade/Iconica/Getty Images; p. 48 Thomas Barwick/Stone/Getty Images; p. 50 The Washington Post/Getty Images; cover and interior pages background images © iStockphoto.com/chaluk.

Designer: Brian Garvey; Photo Researcher: Nicole Baker; Senior Editor: Kathy Kuhtz Campbell